FLYING OVER SONNY LISTON

ALSO BY GARY SHORT

Theory of Twilight

LIMITED EDITIONS
Desire
Looking Past Today

FLYING OVER SONNY LISTON

POEMS BY GARY SHORT

UNIVERSITY OF NEVADA PRESS
RENO   LAS VEGAS

WESTERN LITERATURE SERIES

A list of books in the series appears at the end of this volume.

Winner of the 1996 Western States Book Award for Poetry

The Western States Book Awards are a project of the Western States Arts Federation. The awards are supported by the National Endowment for the Arts and by Crane Duplicating Services.

The paper used in this book meets the requirements of American National Standard for Information Sciences—Permanence of Paper for Printed Library Materials, ANSI Z39.48-1984. Binding materials were selected for strength and durability.

LIBRARY OF CONGRESS
CATALOGING-IN-PUBLICATION DATA

Short, Gary, 1953–
    Flying over Sonny Liston : poems / by Gary Short.
       p. cm. — (Western literature series)
    ISBN 0-87417-285-3 (alk. paper)
    I. Title. II. Series.
    PS3569.H588F57   1996
    811'.54—dc20   96-7761
                                  CIP

University of Nevada Press, Reno, Nevada 89557 USA
Copyright © 1988, 1990, 1991, 1992, 1993, 1994, 1995, 1996
  by Gary Short
All rights reserved
Manufactured in the United States of America

Jacket design by Erin Kirk New

First Printing
05 04 03 02 01 00 99 98 97 96 5 4 3 2 1

for Charlie Buck

We fall, not on our knees, but on our hearts,
A posture humbler far and more downcast.

—Vassar Miller

CONTENTS

i

FROM THE GROUND

PSALM

The sky is the red of the healing wound
of St. Agatha. New light
cast on the seven dead geese
stacked in the bed of the truck.
Their wings stiff around their bodies
make them cocoons of former flight.

The boy's breath, like a white wing,
hangs in the air above him.
His ears pink with wind,
the steel ridges of the truck bed
stripe his jeans with cold.
The sleeping dog rides in the back with him.
He can hear his father & two uncles
in the cab laughing. Their heads bob
between the guns on the rack.

On some of the geese the eyes are open.
A nonliving eye not quite clear,
like the clouded face of a watch.
He thinks of flying, how it would feel
to have nothing surround you.

You can hear their call
long before you see them.
He remembers hearing a flock
on another morning. Geese
stitched across the gray cloth of sky
just before the sun rose
red over the uneven mountains.

The birds flying over a boy's sleep,
distant voices lifting up memories—
the lull of silence after the rodeo, the bull
grazing with the clown's pony.
The grain sack full with struggling rabbits
slung over his shoulder, their vigorous feet
pounding his back as he walked
to the Saturday stock auction.
That distant call
made him want to be good.

The truck rattling over a cattleguard startles
the boy alert & he hears a moan.
At first he thinks it's the dog,
dreaming after birds.
But then another drone releases
from one of the geese.
He had watched them fall, spin around
& crumple like a kite in a dive,
dying in midair.

He sorts through the bodies,
black heads, pliant collared necks,
plush silvered breasts piled
limp & ruffled. He finds the goose
& holds it, unfolds the shut wings.
In the soft rush
of riffled feathers he feels
the clotted blood where shot entered.

Opening the black visors of the bill,
he covers the nose holes with his fingers
& blows a few breaths of air
into the silty hollow of the bird.

And the dead bird gives back
the boy's own breath
in distinct syllables, nasal & conversational,
before the bill goes slack.
Then the boy breathes harder into the goose,
cradles it & listens

until there is music, a swell of air
returned over the bird's vocal chords, a purr,
a dirge, a lost-soul quaver.
A blue cone of sound, human-made,
or made human.

LITTLE MAKEWEIGHTS OF GUILT

I handed Clayton the shotgun, my arms
heavy with what I'd given up.
"You hold the light," he said.
Randy filled the stolen fire extinguisher
with paint thinner we'd found in the barn,
& we walked under a sliced moon to find the tree.

We stepped on the barbed wire,
pulled a strand up to trespass through.
"Hold the light, hold the damn light," they said.
The gun barrel gleamed toward stars.
We came to the oak, listened
for the life inside.

I thought of the queen
hidden within the tree.
The flashlight felt cold in my hands,
the beam too focused.
Clayton's flannel shirt, dark blue diamonds
within light blue diamonds.

The click of the safety catch lifted.
Then quick fire & the bark blasted open to hive,
a waxen aorta massed with bees.
The pressured poison bathed the hive, the bees
sparking in white lather, & heavier honey
trickling down the trunk in strings.

GATHERING

All night the bent apple trees
drop their fruit in the storm,
& I don't hear one fall, not one.

What else fell while I slept?

The twisted limbs glitter silver
in the early sun. A blur of bees
dizzy among broken apples on the ground.

At first waking I'm confused
& mistake the busy dance
as warm blossoming,

when the bees need nectar & the flowers
need pollen to be moved. I think
that's how it works, but
I admit to confusion

about the sexual affinity
of apple trees & bees.

These bees swarm the full-grown overripe fruit.
They are drawn
to sweetness. I have known for a long time

the seduction of an apple.
In fourth grade I shared my snack of graham crackers
& quartered apple with Adrian Vucinich.

To impress her, I would bite the crackers into outlines
of states, accepting requests—
Idaho, Illinois,
the difficult shape of Texas.

I know
it was only the love of a small boy,

but a small thirst
accumulates, as I've learned again from the sparrows
that sip this morning from pocket mirrors of water
in the hoofprints of cattle.

NEAR THE BRAVO 20 BOMBING RANGE

I bring the mare a green apple & then we ride
the wrinkled land along the river road
in the slow-turning wheel of the day.
Past the pen of the brown goat with a broken moan,
past the stiff glove thick with dirt
where it has lain on the path since winter,
past the coyote slung over the barbed fence,

its eyes gone to sky—
blue where a black jet angles
high above the stand of aspen, leaves
spinning to coin in the wind's hand.
I ride past the green wave of alfalfa
that grows one sweet inch each day.

Over the next mountain is the range,
public land bombed for thirty-five unauthorized years.
At what point is turning back an option?
The skeleton of a mustang, dreaming its run,
rises slowly back out of dust.

Farther out, the surface of the marsh is sunstruck tin.
The ones who walked here before
walked quietly & believed the green
slick on the pond.
I hear the jet after it is gone.
What remains—a white strand, sheer against the sky,
with the breath of the mare
as she bends to drink
from the still water.

BIRDS

With our hands we shaped awkward birds
from the mud

of the shallow creek, & one
clumpy Jesus left to dry

in the ruddy April sun.
My brother showed me

how to put my thumbs together, cup
my hands, & give my breath to them

until I made the call
of the mourning dove, fleshy

& sad. When we came back to the creek,
we couldn't find

the clumsy birds or blessed figure
among the lumps of clotted dirt.

Pennies we tossed in the murky water
sank with the weight of our wishes

& settled with the stones
into a future

we did not know—

TIDINGS

Bitterness will flow
The earth will burn
   —from a Mayan prophecy

The bloated carcass of a wild horse
is not abstraction
but a specific example—

the cyanide that seeps into the creek
from heaps of dirt leached for microscopic gold,
its residue. The death of a mustang,
wind bristling a fetlock's stiff hair,
is a political statement.

Bitterness will flow

There are well-funded scientists
in a lab in California who breed weapons
delivered & unleashed at the Test Site
near cloud-shadowed Yucca Mountain.
A clacking train shakes the dreams
of a child in Fernley, Nevada.

Waking, she looks out the window. Her breath,
a quivering cell on the cold glass,
grows & then shrinks.
The bow on her white-sheep nightgown
is tied to sign for infinity.
She hears the lurching

boxcars full of harm
now past her. She cannot see
the steel tracks glint on & off in moonlight,

silvery rills of a stream
that runs to the vanishing point . . .

the earth will burn

CHURCH

Her eyes are half-closed in prayer,
& her face shines
with the light that falls
through the stained-glass window above her,
where Mary gathers the dead body of Jesus
into her arms & holds him against her body.
The religious air smells of smoke & wood.
I am twelve & she is two years older
& lives in the next town,
but I have watched her Sunday by Sunday
become a woman. I try to hear her voice
in the petitions voiced in unison.
Her face seems smooth as glass
like the face of the woman in the book
beneath white handkerchiefs
in my father's dresser drawer.

When I went looking for dark socks for church,
I found it. The book titled
Erotic Wisdom of the Orient.
Under the book is a letter
folded in half. It is
from my father to my mother,
written in thick, black ink
on unlined paper. He says
that he has made mistakes
& that he does not want to lose her.

The book has illustrations
of women & men
in many different positions.

There is one woman, a courtesan
according to the caption,
who has neatly folded
her pink kimono on the bamboo chair.
She is on her knees & elbows,
& a man enters her from behind.
she has thin ankles, & her toes curl.
Her black hair is pinned up.
Her eyes half-closed & reverent.

I look & see
my parents in the pew hold hands & pray.
My father's dark socks are too big for me
& bunch at the tongues of my scuffed shoes.
Why is the paper hidden there
deep in my father's drawer—has he
never given her the note?
Maybe sex is a kind of prayer.
I do want to touch you, he wrote.

ONE SUMMER

Mother returns from the orchard.
She's made a basket of her blue
& white checked apron
full of apples streaked with color
like the dusk sky, & sweet.
Each with a short stem
to twist & make a wish on
the first letter of a girl's name.

A wish. The girl is from the city,
visiting her aunt & uncle down the road.
On hot days we float a makeshift raft,
made of lashed boards,
out to the middle of the lake.
Late July her shoulders ache with sunburn.
I rub lotion into her peeling skin
& move close to let my lips graze her neck.
She'll be going home soon.

On a muggy evening, my father gets drunk
& staggers past the hissy geese
to feed the two pigs.
He throws them eggshells, rinds of melon,
curled & rusted apple skins.
The pigs grow huge on our refuse.
They will be slaughtered in September.
My father strokes their pink ears. He tells them,
"You're the only ones who understand."

I am sixteen,
I don't understand
anything. The taste of her kisses
is sweet & deep, but not like apples.
In the backseat
under a leaf of moon,
she takes my hand
to her belly & makes me trace
the scar of the C-section
where seven months before
the boy was slipped out—one first & last look
at the baby, slick & shining with her blood,
before they took him away.

OUT OF NIGHT

Frightened by the figures
she had drawn that day, the child hurries
through the black hallway

to her mother's room & curls to
the blanket of warm body. Two breaths
in the house.

The wind had risen
& begun to trouble the chime
in the linden tree, the ringing

in the girl's mind
like clothes hangers clicking
against each other,

bodies in the closet, faces
with huge warped mouths
& unsettling eyes.

Hold me, the child says, hold me,
& her mother wakes in cold shadow,
in the hour's unlit mouth,

& they hold to each other
in the wind-surrounded house, holding tight
until the sun comes up, round

& yellow as the child would draw it,
its bright, scrawled yellow
running beyond the circled outline,
an inexact & blinding reply.

ELEGY FOR MY MOTHER
Aldora Joyce, 1922–1993

The sunflower
all day long follows
    the light
    (heaven's eye)
& even after its star has set,
continues to look out
                until loss

is realized, & then
it can only stare into the ground.
    The last time
    she visited,
we walked barren hills at dusk.
Puffs of dust rose up around our feet,
                   settled

back to dust
where our long shadows
    spired.
    Pain is heavy
& our skins are thin,
why we need the word "mercy,"
                as we heard

the Victory Baptist Choir sing
one Sunday in Sacramento,
    my mother & I
    walking by.
She pulled me in
among that bright noise while they sang,
              Have mercy, have mercy.

Under the four-paned window
cut high up on the wall,
I wake
    & try
to count the stars
in each framed square of sky,
            try to

replace her, star
by star. The moon's
      thin yellow
      like a petal
or a butterfly wing pinned
against black velvet.
          There's the ticking

of the wood stove. Wind
twists smoke from the chimney.
      The dead are not
      the sound of wind
as someone once wrote,
they are the sound of smoke.
         White ash

lifts like contrary snow
into the day's brightening
      where the dark
      peels away.
The stars join
(have mercy) an enlarging
         light.

II
FALLEN LIGHT

THE STARS THAT FELL

We brought home a thousand green-white stars
& two moons in a box from the five-and-dime . . .
my father lifting me up to place them,
gum-backed, fluorescent, on my bedroom
ceiling's zig-zag cracks. In an hour,
my room expanded to universe,
the stars pilfering glow from a lamp.

When the light clicked off, the sudden stars
stayed on, five-pointed & bright.
Random constellations
my parents & I had affixed to the ceiling,
new gods scattered above me.

But with the lights off,
it was the opposite of real night;
the stars would dim
in darkness, not remain as dependable guides,
their brief show dissolved
into the clear chimes of the mantel clock.

As I got older, the stars,
one by one, lost their hold, wrinkled
& fell, a hole left
where light had been. The reverse
of what my parents had told me
about people becoming stars when they die.

Each blank place
corresponded to a new death—
Crystal Kent, my classmate killed in a car wreck;

Bobby Porter's mother; the murdered president;
my grandfather. Each
a brightness, fading.

Until I couldn't stand the point-by-point loss
& stripped the remainder off,
my fingertips rubbed tender
in their futile attempt to take back
the map I had cast & learned.

VESPERS

A linnet pulls a tuft of cowhair
snarled on barbed wire.
The threads of hair shine red-gold
in her beak. She flies into last light.

At the horizon, earth & sky
reach a truce. The sun just down,
barn swallows tumble in the afterglow
above the slow-turning windmill.
The hill darkens,

a saddle rubbed with oil,
not yet the complete black of Nevada night.
There's the soft whickering of a horse,
the flames of a hundred Asian poppies nodding red,
then the descending quiet.

WHITE

She had told no one.
She was playing solitaire.
I read the morning paper.
My father, outside,
brought cordwood to the house
in a blue wheelbarrow.

There was the slick sound
of a playing card
on the maple table, a slap
that signaled a finality.
I glanced up & met
the blue eyes of my own beginning.

When my mother said, "cancer,"
the word was set upon the whiteness
of accumulating snow.

And when I still didn't understand,
she asked me to touch it,
her mortal secret.

Modest, we both turned away
while my fingers felt the knot,
all that remained of my mother's breast.

"Don't tell your father. Don't tell."
Outside the window the snow
fell, a vow of silence,
white ashes.

No one, neither doctor
nor husband, had touched this.
She had been alone
with her body for a long time.

The only sound
was the snap of wood
in the fireplace, the blue flame
burning.

I'd been reading about a woman
lost on a remote road in Nevada.
The rancher who found her body
in deep, soft snow
remarked about the silence
that was everything.

She'd worked the swing shift,
serving drinks at the Gold Dust Casino,
borrowed a Willie Nelson tape
& drove out in the storm alone.

Enjoying the music,
the getting away, she went too far.
High-centered in the new snow,
the car stalled.

At dawn she set out to walk back
in the continuous snowfall,
one more cold thing in a cold land.
To her it may have seemed
she was dying of all that whiteness,
not of cold. She grew tired

& lay down in the perfect white.
And the snow fell
until she was covered
with quiet.

GENTLE

My mother, dying, observes her fifty-year
marriage, says, "We could have been
more gentle with each other." And I watch
my father slumped in a chair by her bed,
reaching finally, when she gives in to sleep,
to touch her hand pale against the white sheet.

There's a quiet, like water calming.

On a picnic thirty years ago,
I sit on a yellow bedspread
fitting black olives on each of my fingers.
A more formal time, my mother
wears a blue voile dress & high heels
that aerate the soft dirt
near the shore at Fallen Leaf Lake.
When my parents begin to argue,
I chew the olives from one hand
& measure the fight
with what I call "the fuck-you meter."
My middle finger extended, the virtue
of the needle—honed
by their unfairness to each other, pointing

toward my mother when she
sneers something mean, swinging back
to my father as he swears,
then bolts away & leaps,
landing hard in the little rented boat
that recoils & wobbles.
The wake from the oars slaps the shore. My father's

manic rowing takes him quickly
to the center of the lake.

My mother, unable to swim, cannot reach him.
She stands at the edge
& shouts, "You come here now!"
"No," he taunts, "Why
don't you come *here?*"

The lake is a squint of bright blue.
In their rage, I am forgotten but struck
by the ache. If he looked back from the boat,
did he see her as I do?

In that blue dress & with her red hair blazing,
she is new fire advancing like flame
on the parked Impala
immaculate with his care.
The shining chrome winces in glaring light.

Her freckled ankles tapered
to patent heels made meaningful
with anger—she kicks hell
out of the polished white car.

I can't say for sure if it was that day
or another, but I remember my mother
removing a brittle monarch butterfly caught
in the glittering grillwork of the Chevrolet.
She fanned out the lifeless wings,
straightened the bent eyelash legs,
& brought it home in her high-heeled shoe.

There was reconciliation.
I saw my father touch her, try
to smooth the sleeve of her dress
as if it were flesh. The water
on the lake rippled
where they went out in the boat together.
Rings on the surface broken like oaths,
as I lobbed rocks
at a duck impossibly far from shore.

Distance makes my parents small.
One yellow leaf of silence
falling as I walked to the car
that my mother punished.

I rubbed my hand over the heel-pocked door,
each indented half-moon
the size of a fingertip, my own.

DUST

There is dust on everything in Nevada
   —William Stafford

Dust settles on clocks, accumulates
& clings like boredom. There is gray dust
blurring bedroom mirrors, gilded dust swirling
in pieces of sunlight
falling through the broken ceiling,
& the waltz of dust on the floor
of the condemned dance hall.
Dust silvers fingertips holding an old book.
Dust on piano keys, on white tablecloths,
windowsills, bare lightbulbs
that now throw a dusty yellow light.
Dust that sleeps under a blanket of dust.
Dust dulling the rust-freckled barbed wire,
fallen down, keeping out no one, keeping no one in.
Wind dervishes the desert, & there is dust
thick as thirst in a cowboy's throat.
After a flurry, dust is the calm
   on everything:
in the ocher of a dry riverbed, a lizard
scribbles his tail in dust; dust fills the tracks
& denies that coyote passed this way;
a sun-bleached dust furs cow skulls.
There is the dust of the dead—
& in winter, snow,
the cold shadow of dust.

WOVOKA

(1856–1932)
for Carole Maso & Duane Slick

At his grave I find offerings—
a horseshoe, some oddly shaped blue pebbles,
& the thin bones & skull of a crow
sucked clean by God & devoted flies.

The horseshoe will sink into
its own impression, settle finally
into the dirt until only the idea
of the horseshoe will remain.

A living crow
is perched on a moon-colored stone.
It lifts, a shadow unfolding
over seven bleached hills of dust
toward Walker River. The bird's wings
are black prisms.

My fingers worry the blue pebbles
worn smooth by the affection of water, worn down
to the river's old truth.
I let the pebbles drop as measures

at the grave of Wovoka,
who dreamed the Ghost Dance & believed
if his people danced long & hard enough
the dead would live again.

When men from other tribes came to him,
they asked for proof of his vision.
Wovoka took off his hat

& invited them to look inside it.
Some saw only darkness
inside an empty hat, but some saw
the whole spirit world.

I stand & turn
in the four directions of this world,
as though purpose
supposes what ought to be seen.
One man's dream in the bowl of a hat.

The vision I want to see is in the distance
that does not end.
I have come to haunt the dead.

OUTSIDE

Some strings of light.
Mostly absence.
Out the window, trees,
the narrow margin. The edges
carved in new sun.

I sway,
stalled at the warm window.
Out there the sweep of wings.
Out there wind's tangle.

I sway to the absence,
a disappearance like hushed flight.
Now the wind nods slack with sleep.

In the tree outside my window,
the scurry of wings
like a preface to arrows.

Latticed shadows of limbs
weave a net of the day.
The sway of the tree I depend on
to summon me.

RAIN
—RJS, 1941–1980

This rain is not consolation.
The rain is lawless.
In the near-dark, I light a candle.
The flame a fluttering goldfish tail

which I saw in the mortuary garden pond
before my brother's funeral.
Teased by rain, mistaking
the first disturbance of raindrops

for the spattering
of a fist of scattered food,
a goldfish will rise to the surface
to find nothing.

White wax gutters down
& hardens on the dark
grain of the table.

Dying, my brother's fingers
were thin white candles.
His skin

not like rain
but like snow. So silent.
His body glowed, the cells slowly
flaring out.

It is his last day.
I watch him sleep. A death-drowse.
His thin fingers touch
his penis, belly, chest,
& his face, as if

he is trying to memorize
himself.

GIVEN BACK

All things are doubled
at dusk at Fulkerson Slough, reflected,

given back—clouds, birds,
my love for you. The gold of leaves

becomes too pure, too heavy,
falls in drifts.

On the long horizon the moon appears
a carpenter's blue thumbnail. In this quiet

the sun closes
its simple knot. It is dark

by the time we cross into the old graveyard.
We try to read the markers

but can't discern dates or names.
With your fingers you find the outline

of an etched figure. "It's a lamb," you say.
We are silent,

thinking we know what this might mean.
Your fingers are still scented from sprigs

of sage we picked today.
I lean into you & think

of home, the gardenia petals soaking
in a white dish.

HARD WINTER

While we slept
        the snow
increased & made the world seem far away.
     I'd wake
with one cheek warm against the sheet, the other
     cold as an anvil. Snow
drifted up & sloped
against the weathered house.

A few miles off the highway with
     four feet of piled white,
              we had no way out
     until Mack
who lived at the mountain's base, dozed up
in his 1938 Cat. Mack
worked the gears while his wife
     stood behind him, her hands
     around him, his shoulders
     draped with her Shoshone-black hair.
In her mouth she tendered a strip of leather.

The high snow moved,
my father held out ten bucks,
            but Mack
waved him off, said,
     "You wouldn't
happen to have any whiskey, would you?"
And he shut the dozer down,
bragging about its good stack

& came inside
to drink & show us a pouch full of crystals

that he & his wife had dug from the red dirt
        in summer.
She didn't say anything, she
                        never did.
We'd tried asking her name before
& were embarrassed to ask again.
My dad called her, Mack the Wife.

When they left
                my mother gave Mack's wife
                the ten-spot,
& she slipped it into a flannel pocket.
        Afterward, my dad said,
"Mack would be happy with just the whiskey."
        Mom said,
"They need the money."
        Dad shoved a wedge of pine
        in the woodstove, & it rasped
        against burnt logs that dropped ash
        & crackled, muffling his mumbled,
"So do we."

With the road cleared,
                I could walk out
in the jeweled cold
                & follow
the split-heart tracks of starving deer.
        In the morning
the valley I entered was a cradle of silence

where light from the winter sun was thin
        & slanted. Wind rushed down
        from Hole-in-the-Mountain
sounding like the river that wasn't there.

Ice would glitter silver,
shiver & break away from bare aspen limbs.

There was a house tucked in snow
where a girl & her father lived.
I could see her
                    in the window,
        Her hair
shone red as I walked by
hoping she would notice me.
                                    And when she didn't
I retraced my steps
                    in the snow,
        backwards,
so that she wouldn't know
I had already passed her house.
                                    When she
finally looked up to see, I waved
        as if to say
I just happened by, never mind
these footprints in front of me.

Then came the last big snow.
        Early April,
soon there'd be snowmelt,
& my dad & I would have to hike
        up above the road,

plunge midthigh in mud
to dig a ditch & divert the runoff.
        One late afternoon
Mack & his wife showed again
        to plow us out.

They came inside. My father poured,
set the whiskey on the table.

Mack was excited. He'd seen
        three wild horses
        in the draw & they looked healthy.
        A few weeks earlier
        he'd left hay bales for them.
He ran his fingers around the shot glass rim,
        & said the mining company
had hired him on to push some dirt.
"What do they have planned
for this mountain?" my father asked.
Mack's hands
            slipped to his lap.
"Tear it all to hell," he said.

It was a last frozen moment
        of that winter.
My mom & dad, Mack
                    & his wife
quiet around the kitchen table.
It had been a hard winter for everything.
        My mother said
that they should stay for dinner.
My father poured another glass for Mack

        then turned.
        I remember
how he faced the dusk outside,
        drifted snow
& the twisted cottonwood erased
in the darkening mirror of window.

III

BELIEF OF SKY

EROTICA

A Basque sheepherder, sixty autumns
& so many leaves ago,
trailed the flock of his own confusing needs
to a Nevada isolation
& made his camp in the aspen grove, scaled yellow
with leaves that shivered even in stillness
or what he took for calm.

We've made our way up the steep path to look
at the sheepherder's erotica
carved into the white bark of the tree—
the naked outlines of an aroused man & woman
originally drawn a few inches apart
in anticipation, desire like a dark scar

shaped in bark. As the years
encircled one another like a target
& the tree girth widened,
the lines extended
& the figures moved closer & met.
A simple reaching after contact
but its context a continuance,
the tree's promise
of two people grown into each other.

At least until the tree
is eighty years old or so,
& then the bark will peel
its cicatrix of pornography
& the two figures fold, ghostlike.

Our legs ache from the climb.
We stand, each in our own outline,
as we have stood in a candle-lighted room
waiting to touch. The shadows on the wall
magnified & echoed,
shadow outside other shadows
trying to break the boundary
of our human shape.

SHOSHONEAN

Every thing that roamed this world
had a song of its own.

The sky was something to be thought about.
Way out this way. Way out that way.

Black night. Black night.
This was on Coyote Lung Mountain,

when animals & humans
spoke the same language.

Blackbird, black seed, black obsidian bead.
And all things echoed

like an owl's call in the black night,
every thing that roamed this world.

I myself am going back, he said.
Going back, he said.

Blackbird. Black night.
I myself am going back,

back to Coyote Lung Mountain.
Way out this way. Way out that way.

NAMING

I hadn't crawled into the attic
to take down boxes with their fur of dust
& search for the painted wood cutouts
that had hung on the wall when I was a boy—
the cat with the fiddle,
the dish & spoon with lanky legs, the cow
that jumped over the smiling moon.
I tried to picture you
looking up at those same figures on the wall.
Your mother & I had not yet bought clothes or toys.
When she miscarried
five months away from your birth,
you were still daydream
& speculation. This evening
I want to tell you
about when I was a boy & my mother called
across the pasture—*Scarlet, Stormy,*
Crystal—& the three bays came in a canter
to break carrots with their great teeth
& to have us pat their hard & heavy heads.
When I was a boy it seemed the world
was brought forth from naming & desire,
the way wildflowers showed
in April when my father pointed
& gave them names & formal life—*jewel flower,*
coltsfoot, shooting star.
And when we called out the names of birds,
as quick as we could say
flicker or *swift,*
they would fly away, shrinking

from sight. And you, gone too,
gone with the birds who flew from naming
into the blue belief of sky.

AMERICAN LIGHT

I watched the distant explosions.
The bursting bombs struck matches
in the night, brief flares
beyond the bedroom window. *Who's there?*
My mother said it wasn't anything—
a practice bombing on the Bravo Range,
just think of fireworks
on the 4th of July.

I leaned against the cold window,
closed my eyes to a deeper night.
The distant white flashes & the rumble
like a panicked horse running.
Across the hall I could hear my mother
fuss at her hair in the mirror.
She'd put on lipstick & her blue dress
to wait for my father's return from the bar.

Five miles away in town, two searchlights
from the Ford dealership
cut the black sky into angles.
On the highway out of town, burning beyond my sight
& understanding, a red-neon-
pulsing whorehouse heart beckoned
bomber crews from the air force base.

My mother waited, looked out on the long dirt road
for roving headlights to show
among the crowd of lights, seen & unseen.
When the bombing stopped, the stars
seemed brighter, more quiet.

Falling asleep I might have dreamed
the future—Baghdad on fire,

or a Vietnamese girl trying to outrun
her own burning skin.
My mother told me to sleep tight,
not to be afraid.
Where she kissed me good-night,
her lipstick flamed red on my cheek.

THE GIANT ANTS OF TEXAS
Lafcadio Hearn, 1881

"It's like we're inside the pie
& those clouds are the meringue," Mrs. Courtney says.
I can't see the clouds, or rather
myopia makes everything a cloud.

When I was fevered,
Mrs. Courtney left the other boarders
to prepare me tea with the leaves of the pepper plant.
She bathed my bulging eyes with egg white.
I am hungry for touch.

When my wife first undressed
in my presence, to see her
I had to be so near
that my nose grazed her skin—
the ribbed pink lines & ring marks
from her corset. It was
the incense of a strangely new
& beautiful worship.

I have never seen a cloud,
except her, a haziness walking away.
My letters
to an address in Ohio, unanswered.

Once a procession of ants
entered my room through the window.
From an inch away,
the giant architectural ants of Texas
looked like black ink

that had spilled from my pen
onto sheets of white paper.

Tonight my hands trace
my body's imperfect history.
The scars, not seen but felt,
like pain remembered.
Perhaps Mrs. Courtney
will bring breakfast, call "Son."

I remember my mother would leave ribbons
on the pecan limbs that scratched
the lens of my bedroom window
—pink, green & red, for the wren
to find & weave into its cup of a nest.
The little bird would claim the ribbon,
chirp & puff up & then dart away,
the thin banner blurring in its beak.
The sky received the wren into a wide silence.

I grew up in a house of shadows:
I knew ghosts.
If this life is quick light
between two long darknesses,

then I am lonely.
I hear the wren's absence & feel
the shadow of a huge cloud
crossing the moon, the shadow
so cold, complete.
And then there is no moon,
no light to fall through.

FLYING OVER SONNY LISTON

Sonny Liston is on all fours,
trying to rise, a flame of pain
in the center of his head.

The crowd noise blurs,
then distances, as though he is shut
in a room by himself.

In his face there is silence.
His skin glistens with sweat,
& the glare & flurry of camera flashes

are far-away lights in his eyes.
Cassius Clay thin & sharp, stands
above him, arms a recited W.

The airplane rises over the cemetery
where Liston is buried
next to the runway at McCarran Airport.

What I recall is his bad press—
how he learned to box in prison,
how he hung out with the worst people.
His violence & his size,

a film clip of him
sullenly jumping rope
to a record of "Night Train."

A woman in a pink blouse sits next to me.
Her fingers try to memorize a thick crucifix
on a chain around her neck.

She's nervous. But from this safe distance,
looking out the oval window
& beyond the wing, I see the cross
of the airplane shadowing grave sites.

A boxer knows momentum
can suddenly shift. One blow
changes everything.
The plane lifts. Closing my eyes, I hear

the referee's eight-count, the knockout signaled.
Liston is out of time & still on his knees,
suffering & silent, "Inarticulate

in the way we all are," James Baldwin wrote,
"when more has happened to us
than we know how to express."

In eight seconds an aircraft can bank into
& fly through fists of clouds
above the city of Las Vegas
& the grave of Sonny Liston.

He died alone in a motel room.
His life was nothing like mine,
& so we share a solitariness,

like the passengers on this plane who rise
or fall together
& individually, each with defeats.
The fight for survival is the fight.

IN THE GRADUAL

When I hugged Nana
she smelled like sour books, old.

But there are no books.
There is a dresser drawer
filled with flat, stacked tinfoil,
& there are Mason jars
to the brim with rubber bands—

red, brown, & green.
A startled red parrot stitched
on the sofa pillow.

The day we brought her home
I sat in the back seat of the car
with her. She knew me
but pointed to my father
& asked, "Who is that man?"
I didn't answer, but my mother
turned, reached for her hand
& told her the man was her son.
She didn't believe us, but was quiet.

In the backyard
the lime tree's shadow lengthened.
I had a bat, rough
& nicked. I tossed
the limes in air
& hit them as they fell.
Hit right, it was a pure sound—
the split peeling, juice spraying
from the small fruit

sent flying over the roof.

Nana watched
from the upstairs window,
& I didn't know
if she knew me. I hit
a lime that didn't clear
the roof, but caught
up there, lodged against the chimney.
I looked to the window
& her face was gone.

At dinner I could tell she'd been sleeping,
her cheek dotted red with chenille.
She grabbed my wrist.
I was her cousin Harold,
dead in the flu epidemic in 1919.
I looked at her flesh hand,
wrinkled white crepe.

Later my mother said
to hug Nana good-night.
I went to her & she whispered,
"Sleep, Harold. Sleep."

The baseball bat leaned against the bedboard,
bits of lime peel & pulp packed into
the tiny cracks of the wood.
The Coca-Cola bottle on the shelf
gleamed full of dimes, & the citrus
smell, well-hit limes, the dry grass,
Nana's eyes, alone,
olive green & watching.

WATCHING THE AX FALL

There was the crack of the wood—

the sound delayed,
unlike now when first the leaves rattle,
a door slams shut somewhere in the house,
& then I feel the wind.

Nothing is completed, not even thought.
Starlings swirl
& climb a spiral of air,
then as one body & at a certain tilt,
        disappear.

This morning there were new tulips abruptly red,
vestment red, & morning glories

blossoming. Snowflakes in my father's hair
when he walked that winter out to the woodpile
behind the barn.
In a photograph on the end table,
he's in uniform. Once he told me
about Paris after the war
& a carousel of brightly painted cows.

Sunfall, a blade of light slices the Sierras.
My father, small & afraid, in his hospital bed.
The cold rails of the bed. The wind.

The cows all face the flesh sun.
The horse is eating dropped fruit in the orchard
where century trees bend.

The eyes of the cattle reflect
what is outside them. If you looked you would see
the night leaning against the barn
collapsed on itself.

A NEW KIND OF DELICATE
for *Charlie Buck*

Tracks of two people
walking in new snow.
The snow blurred & blue
under the tin winter moon
where they stopped to hold each other

good-night. Then the tracks part,
though his footprints reveal a turning back
toward her, a hesitation
& then a return on alone

past the whitening field
where the donkey stands
beneath a pine, its breath
hovering between the comical ears
as if the donkey had an idea.
A bowed branch of the pine
is a grin of snow.

The man walks up his road,
following the beacon of his porch light home.
Arriving at the door,
he looks up against the light
& sees a lacy pentacle.
At first he's unsure

of what it is. It looks like
the trace of a huge snowflake.
A glittering gauze of snow
clings to thread.

He stands under the web. He believes
the donkey is still in the field, still thinking.

This is a different kind of delicate.
Not like the nail
that scrapes your secret. More like
finding something promising in the garden
in early summer. A gentle tug

separates the radish from the mud.
He stands for several moments of silence.
The spiderweb trembles in the wind
but does not break.

It does not break. This is
a tender storm
that doesn't tear a spiderweb,
that leaves what is beautiful intact.

DRIVING NEVADA/REPRISE

Silence is the horizon
where air's a tremor, & the town I think I see
is an old fold of layering heat.
My grip on the steering wheel relaxes.
The radio signal clots with static, but
it is all right. Up ahead
in the distance that becomes time,
a jukebox in the Mozart Club in Goldfield
booms Merle Travis. It is all right
& I am happy. That the windshield
can't hold all the sky.
That when one goes to a clear place
the mind will sometimes follow.
I am glad to be driving because
so often I have been left behind. But today
I'll listen to a song in the Mozart Club
& then drive a long way toward the horizon
          while the hours
huddle like a reverent herd of cattle
praying to the great grass-god.

FOUND IN ANY GRAY

Because there was a ship in a bottle
on the table next to a grainy gray photograph,
I asked Perilee Jardell, our new neighbor,
about the young man in the photo. She said,
"That's Delbert, my son. He was lost at sea."
She said this in the soft way adults talk
when they don't think children will understand,
or when they don't want children to understand.
   I thought
that Delbert had gone away & that
he was on a boat or an island,
& he had sent the ship in the bottle as a gift.

I knew I shouldn't ask about her son,
because it made her sad. But I questioned
my parents & asked & asked,
if Delbert was lost,
then why couldn't he be found? Until finally
one night at dinner, my father
motioned no with a sweep of his arm, as if
some things were farther away than I could know.
He told me that years before
Delbert had *taken his own life—*
a phrase more confusing to me
than *lost at sea.* I remember

sitting in my favorite climbing tree.
It was an old cottonwood. Before I was born a bolt
of summer lightning had split the brittle bark
& made a wishbone out of it. From the Y
of the tree I looked past

the green waves of alfalfa
breaking against the sun & wind
& said softly to myself,
in affirmation not despair,
Take your own life, take your own life.

During my visits with Perilee,
I'd sink back in the deep armchair
in that room where I first learned
that people are here & then gone—a husband dies,
& an only child can walk into the ocean & disappear.
Mostly we talked about Artie, the cocker spaniel,
who slept on the floor & half-opened an eye
each time we said his name.

One night I had a dream about the ship in the bottle.
Wild waves of wind lashed the house,
& in sleep the Nevada range became an ocean.
I saw the ship in the bottle bobbing out on the sea
far from any shore, & I knew that the air in the bottle
was Delbert's last breath, preserved all these years,
as though he had gulped one final breath & held it
forever. And that as long as the bottle did not sink,
Delbert would not die. When I woke
in the morning there were leaves on the sea-green lawn,
scattered like feathers of ocean birds, feathers
that fell from out of my dream.

So I never asked Perilee about the ship in the bottle,
& I didn't ask her about Delbert, although
she might mention him—how he was good with horses
or that he had a voice that belonged on radio.
Left alone for a few minutes in the room,

I moved to the framed photo.
The glass in the frame was clean
with the lemon scent of dusting spray.
I held the picture in front of me, held it
close enough to find a breath, & looked
into the gray of his eyes.
I could see, in reflection,
my face in his. Spokes of light
emanated from tiny stars deep in his eyes.

He had become part of the sea,
& he could be raised up like water by the sun.
He could be a cloud drifted landward
to be returned as rain.
If he was lost,
then he might be found
on the gray blank of ocean
out beyond where waves
wreck against the rocks,

or in the first gray of early morning
above silent pastures
& the large sleep of horses
that stand stalwart & blue in the fields.
I began my search many years ago that day,
& I look for him & find him still
anywhere, in any distance,
in any gray.

ACKNOWLEDGMENTS

The author offers grateful acknowledgment to the editors of publications in which poems in this volume previously appeared, some in slightly different form: *Antioch Review* for "Psalm," "White," "The Giant Ants of Texas," and "Gentle"; *Blue Mesa Review* for "Wovoka"; *Chariton Review* for "Dust" and "Driving Nevada/Reprise"; *Cimarron Review* for "Out of Night"; *5 AM* for "In the Gradual" and "Hard Winter"; *Hayden's Ferry Review* for "Outside" and "Rain"; *Interim* for "Found in Any Gray"; *Laurel Review* for "A New Kind of Delicate," "Church," and "Given Back"; *Passages North* for "Flying Over Sonny Liston"; *Provincetown Arts* for "Erotica"; *Quarterly West* for "Gathering," "Tidings," and "One Summer"; *Shankpainter* for "Vespers"; and *Writers' Forum* for "Watching the Ax Fall," "Little Makeweights of Guilt," "The Stars That Fell," "Birds," "Elegy for My Mother," "Naming,"and "American Light."

"Near the Bravo 20 Bombing Range" first appeared in *Handspan of Red Earth: An Anthology of American Farm Poems*, ed. by Catherine Lewallen Marconi (University of Iowa Press, 1991), and appeared in *A New Geography of Poets,* ed. Edward Field *et al.* (University of Arkansas Press, 1992).

This book was written with the help of a 1993–95 Wallace Stegner Fellowship at Stanford University. Appreciation also goes to the Fine Arts Work Center in Provincetown and to the Centrum Foundation and the MacDowell Colony for residencies. Thanks to the Nevada State Council on the Arts for grants support.

Many thanks to Talvi Ansel, Jo Ann Beard, Carol Conroy, Cathy French, Dennis Schmitz, and Judy Vollmer for their assistance with this book. And to Burnett and Mimi Miller, Scott Shaddock, and Henry and Wendy Teichert for help along the way.

WESTERN LITERATURE SERIES

Cruising State:
Growing Up in
Southern California
Christopher Buckley

The Big Silence
Bernard Schopen

Kinsella's Man
Richard Stookey

The Desert Look
Bernard Schopen

Winterchill
Ernest J. Finney

Wild Game
Frank Bergon

Lucky 13: Short Plays
about Arizona, Nevada,
and Utah
edited by Red Shuttleworth

The Measurable World
Katharine Coles

Keno Runner
David Kranes

TumbleWords: Writers
Reading the West
edited by William L. Fox

From the Still Empty
Grave: Collected Poems
A. Wilber Stevens

Strange Attraction: The
Best of Ten Years of
ZYZZYVA
edited by Howard Junker

Wild Indians &
Other Creatures
Adrian C. Louis

Bad Boys and
Black Sheep
Robert Franklin Gish

Stegner: Conversations
on History and
Literature
Wallace Stegner and
Richard W. Etulain

Warlock
Oakley Hall

Flying Over Sonny
Liston: Poems
Gary Short